MW01113895

Cover by Ryan Morgan. Images from Vecteezy and Unsplash.

Made in the USA
Middletown, DE
30 June 2022

68173239R00056